MARKET DAYS

From Market to Market Around the World

Concept and Illustrations by
Marti Shohet

Text by Madhur Jaffrey

BridgeWater Books

To Leslie, for starting me on this journey,
to Rudi, for setting me on the path,
to Michael for his love and support—

M.S.

For Robi, of course—

M.J.

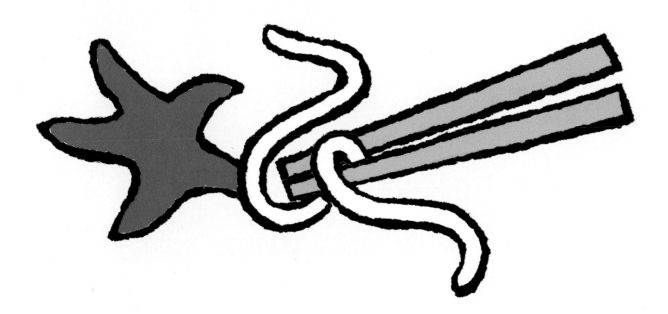

Published by BridgeWater Books, an imprint of Troll
Associates, Inc.

Printed in the United States of America.

10 9 8 7 6 5 4 3 2 1

Library of Congress Cataloging-in-Publication Data
Jaffrey, Madhur.
Market days: from market to market around the world / text by
Madhur Jaffrey; concept and illustrations by Marti Shohet.
    p.   cm.
ISBN 0-8167-3504-2
1. Markets—Juvenile literature.   [1. Markets. 2. Cookery.]
I. Shohet, Marti. II. Title.
HF5470.J34 1995   381'.18—dc20   94-21284

INTRODUCTION

Walking through any marketplace on this globe is a bit like opening a window and looking right into the heart of a country. What people like to buy and sell is easy enough to see. But if you look harder you can also see what people like to laugh at and what fun means to them. You can see that foods that may seem strange in one place are familiar in another. You can see clothes that delight those who wear them, and that ideals of beauty are not the same everywhere. By seeing people stop whatever they are doing to bow down in prayer, you learn the importance of their religions; and by watching how they treat members of their families, you learn what they value. Markets are wonderful places to understand the world.

MARKETS AROUND THE WORLD

North America

Atlantic Ocean

Pacific Ocean

MEXICO

North

West

East

South

South America

HONG KONG

The market in Hong Kong is jammed. Cars honk, passengers hang from double-decker buses, and neon signs blink brightly. Hong Kong is a busy city, old in tradition and modern in looks.

A python is suspended from a hook in the market. It is quite dead but it still curls up and stretches. It will end up as soup. For centuries the Chinese have eaten snake soup in winter. Snake meat keeps them warm.

A man buys a roasted duck that hangs by its neck. With quick, masterly strokes of a cleaver, the shopkeeper cuts it into small, neat pieces.

The Chinese insist on absolute freshness. Long green beans must snap crisply in half and the octopus must still have moving tentacles. Much of the fish is alive and chosen from tanks.

The people of Hong Kong have always enjoyed eating out.
There are restaurants in shopping malls, on boats, and some
right on the pavement. The Chinese eat everything from bears'
paws and bean curd to fish lips and snails, seasoned with
salty soy sauces or pungent ginger or nutty sesame oil. Cooked
dishes are placed in the center of the table and are shared.
The rice is not. Everyone has their own bowl and eats with
chopsticks.

On the pavement, much longer chopsticks are being used
to stir-fry noodles in a wok. Ingredients of many textures—
slippery and crisp, crunchy and soft—are in the wok as well.
Noodles make a good snack. They are always served on
birthdays because they are symbols of long life. That is why
noodles are never cut up but served whole.

EGYPT

The glory of Egypt lies in its silent pyramids, but the excitement of Egypt lies in its bustling bazaars.

"Want to buy a prayer rug?" a hawker cries.

"Out of my way!" yells a boy with caged pigeons.

A woman, her head covered in the Muslim tradition, is tempted by fresh dates, all red, plump, and juicy. Behind her, mud houses stand beside mosques from the 10th century, and narrow winding lanes pass through medieval gates. One such lane specializes in copper pots, another has only onyx, a third glitters with gold. As a break from buying and selling, how about a cup of thick Turkish coffee or sweet minty tea?

There is another market just across the wide Nile River. It has camels for sale. Camels are as important today as they were a thousand years ago. They store fat in their humps and can go without drinking for days. For a country that is mostly desert, no transportation is better. How do you buy a camel? Men wearing *gallabiyahs*, or long robes, spread the camel's lips apart and examine its teeth. This tells them its age. Then they look at the camel's legs. Are they strong? They walk around the camel. Is it good-natured, or might it sit down on a sand dune and refuse to budge?

SENEGAL

The sun is hot in this Senegal market. The women, wearing brightly printed robes called *boubous* and elaborate head wraps, look like creatures from an exotic heaven.

The shoppers here are busy bargaining for colorful cotton fabrics that can be sewn up within the hour, and for fish and peanuts. Peanuts will go into a sauce for chicken, and fish is needed for *cebu jen*, the popular fish stew.

Bargaining is necessary. You ask the price of a fish. The fishwife says, "Ten francs."

You say, "That is too much. I will pay three francs."

The fishwife shrugs. "That is too little. Pay me seven."

You settle on five. Both buyer and seller enjoy this game.

There is a healer in the market. A necklace of chunky amber beads sits grandly around her neck. She pounds and mixes her concoctions in mortars and hollowed out calabashes. She sells dried monkeys' heads to cure disease, and offers wings of owl, ground antelope horns, and monkeys' paws as ways to mend a broken heart.

The women of Senegal love to dress up. For hundreds of years they have beautified themselves by using cosmetics, cleansing creams, and perfumed incense made with woods, oils, grains, and nuts. Smelling good is just as important as looking good, these women say.

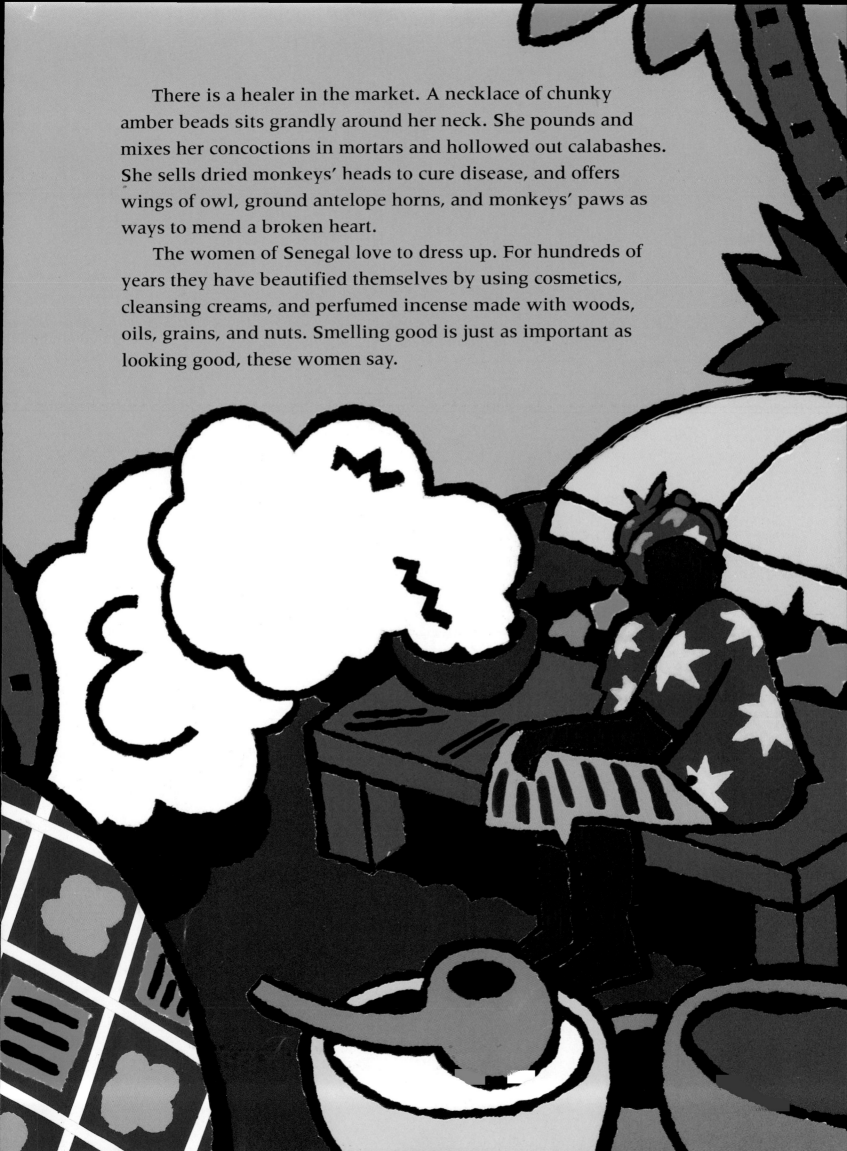

INDIA

For more than three thousand years, the market in the ancient Indian city of Benares has sold silks as soft as butter and cottons as fine as a spider's web. Something even more valuable can be found here as well. This noisy, crowded city is a wise old city, and those who come here to watch and listen can have some wisdom passed on to them.

They can see all of life here and many of God's creatures as well. Camels bring in vegetables from the fields, sacred cows munch on leftover foods, barking dogs chase rickshaws, and donkeys carry loads of bricks. Women in bright saris shimmering with gold thread wear *tikas*, or sacred red dots, on their foreheads. They sell flowers for weddings and funerals. Nothing is hidden here, neither life nor death.

There is color everywhere—in the flowers the women wear, the bright turbans on the men's heads, and in the blue, green, and gold bangles that sparkle in the sunlight. All women wear bangles, not only because they are pretty but because they feel that their arms look like naked bamboo sticks without them.

There is color in the spice shop as well. The yellow of turmeric, the brown of cumin, and the red of the chilies, all of which make Indian food spicy and mouth-watering.

A man sits cross-legged, sipping hot tea with lots of milk and sugar. This tea will make him perspire and cool him off. In India, people will do anything to stay cool.

ITALY

Did you know that freshly baked, crusty bread can be put into salads and soups, or rubbed with olive oil, topped with the ripest of sweet tomatoes, and served at dinner?

They do this in Tuscany, which is the heart of Italy. Here the sun shines with a special brightness, making tomatoes bright red, peppers a deep green, and eggplants a glowing purple. The local market is usually in a medieval town square. Here long salamis and fat cheeses are sold. Indeed, all the ingredients for lovingly prepared family meals can be found here. The market starts at dawn so shoppers have time to return to their kitchens to slice and chop and stir.

By one o'clock, everyone is ready for lunch. It can take four leisurely hours. The whole family is welcome at the neighborhood trattoria. There is red wine from Chianti; bread to be dipped in olive oil; olives with dull green flesh that has to be sucked off the pits; and there are huge portobello mushrooms that are grilled and doused with dressing.

Outside, the sun still shines brightly on the tall cypress trees and vineyards nearby, and the hills topped with old castles in the distance. As the heat builds and the stomach is filled, what else is there to do but to slow down and rest. Even the dog dozes.

MEXICO

Mexicans in the highlands of Chiapas rise at dawn when the hills are still clothed in a chilly mist. Some men carry firewood to market on their backs. Others work in the cornfields. Everyone grows corn. It is a sacred duty. They have been growing corn here for seven thousand years.

The women spend hours weaving. Girls who weave well will surely find worthy husbands. They learn to spin and work the loom when they are just seven years old. Wool from sheep can become a finely brocaded shawl or a blouse, a *huipile,* filled with woven toads and jaguars and designs that show the moving universe. What cloth is not used at home is sold in a nearby market.

The market is in the valley, in a town square dominated by an old Spanish-style church. The church smells of time and incense. Everyone gathers here to meet respected elders, pray, gossip, buy clay pots, and eat. A woman prepares corn tortillas. She takes some corn dough and goes pat, pat, pat, forming a flat tortilla with her practiced hands. She slaps this onto a hot griddle. First, it turns pale and then it starts to puff up. She lifts up the cooked tortilla and throws it into a hollowed gourd lined with cloth. This tortilla will be eaten with beans and washed down with a cup of coffee.

RECIPES FROM AROUND THE WORLD

HONG KONG

Cold Noodles with Peanut Sauce

(Serves 4)

The Chinese like to eat these cold noodles as a first course before the main meal.

1/2 lb (¹/₄ kg) fresh Chinese egg noodles (or spaghetti cooked according to package instructions)
2 tbsp (30 ml) sesame oil
1/4 cup (¹/₁₆ l) peanut butter

1 tbsp (15 ml) peanut oil
1 tbsp (15 ml) soy sauce
2 tsp (10 ml) vinegar
1 tsp (5 ml) sugar
1 scallion
1/4 cup (¹/₁₆ l) water

Bring a large pot of water to a rolling boil. Drop in the noodles and cook until just done. They should retain some crispness. Drain and immediately rinse under cold water. Drain again and put in a bowl. Add 1 tablespoon sesame oil, mix and set aside. Meanwhile, put the peanut butter into a bowl. Slowly add 1/4 cup water, mixing with a wooden spoon. Add the remaining 1 tablespoon sesame oil, peanut oil, soy sauce, vinegar, and sugar. Mix well. Pour over the noodles and toss. Cut the scallion into 2-inch (5 cm) pieces and then cut each piece, lengthwise, into thin strips. Scatter these over the top and serve.

EGYPT

Spice Dip for Raw Carrots

(Serves 6)

This is a dry dip. It is excellent with carrot sticks as well as with celery or cucumbers or cherry tomatoes.

2 tbsp (30 ml) sesame seeds
1 tbsp (15 ml) coriander seeds
2 tsp (10 ml) cumin seeds

1 tbsp (15 ml) kosher salt
Freshly ground pepper
6 raw carrots

Put the sesame seeds, coriander seeds, and cumin seeds in a small, heavy cast-iron frying pan and heat over a medium flame. Keep stirring for 2–3 minutes until the spices give out a roasted smell. Do not let them burn. Let the spices cool a little and then grind them in a clean coffee grinder. Empty into a small bowl. Add the salt and pepper and mix well. Peel the carrots and cut into 3-inch (7 ¹/₂ cm) sticks. Serve with the dip.

SENEGAL
Fresh Papaya
(Serves 2–4, depending upon size)

When you buy a papaya, make sure that it is somewhat yellow and nicely ripe. Serve it for breakfast or as dessert.

1 ripe papaya, slightly soft to the touch
2–4 wedges of lime

Cut the papaya in half or quarters, lengthwise. Remove all the black seeds with a spoon and discard them. Put each piece of papaya on a separate plate with a wedge of lime near it. Squeeze some lime juice over the top. Scoop out the papaya meat with a spoon and eat.

INDIA
Yogurt with Cucumber and Raisins
(Serves 2–4)

You could eat this as a snack or as a salad.

1 tbsp (15 ml) golden raisins
1 cup (¼ l) plain yogurt
1/3 tsp (1 ½ ml) salt
Freshly ground pepper
Half a cucumber

Soak the raisins in hot water for 30 minutes. Drain. Put the yogurt in a bowl with raisins and mix well with a fork until creamy. Add the salt and pepper. Peel the cucumber and grate it into the yogurt. Mix well.

ITALY
Bruschetta
(Serves 4)

You may serve this as a first course or as a snack.

8 slices of fresh, crusty French or Italian white bread
About 3–4 tbsp (45-60 ml) of olive oil
16 fresh basil leaves
1 cup (¼ l) chopped fresh, ripe tomatoes
Salt
Freshly ground pepper

Just before eating, spread the bread slices in front of you on the counter. Brush each with a little olive oil. Put two basil leaves on top of the oil. Put about 2 tablespoons of the chopped tomatoes on top of the basil leaves. Sprinkle a little salt and pepper over the top of the tomatoes and serve.

MEXICO
Tacos
(Serves 2–4)

Here is a complete meal. All that is needed afterward is some fruit.

3/4 cup (³/₁₆ l) canned black beans
4 taco shells
4 tbsp (60 ml) shredded cheese (Cheddar or Monterey Jack)
4 tbsp (60 ml) shredded lettuce
4 tbsp (60 ml) chopped tomatoes
Salt
Freshly ground pepper

Put the beans in a bowl and mash them lightly. Put 3 tablespoons of the mashed beans in each taco shell. Put 1 tablespoon of shredded cheese on top of the beans in each shell. Top the cheese with a tablespoon each of the lettuce and then the tomatoes. Sprinkle a little salt and pepper on the tomatoes and serve immediately.